It may be sunny or cloudy.
It may be rainy or snowy.

Weather and Clouds

Clouds are clues about the weather. Puffy clouds may mean nice weather.

Measuring Weather

Orlando Austin New York San Diego Toronto London

Visit *The Learning Site!*
www.harcourtschool.com

Kinds of Weather

Weather is what the air outside is like. The air may be warm or cool.

Gray clouds may mean rain or snow.

Weather and You

Weather can change from day to day. It is important to dress for the weather.

Measuring Temperature

You can find out how warm the air is. Thermometers measure temperature.

Measuring Rain

Put a rain gauge outside.

The gauge shows how much rain falls.

Measuring Wind

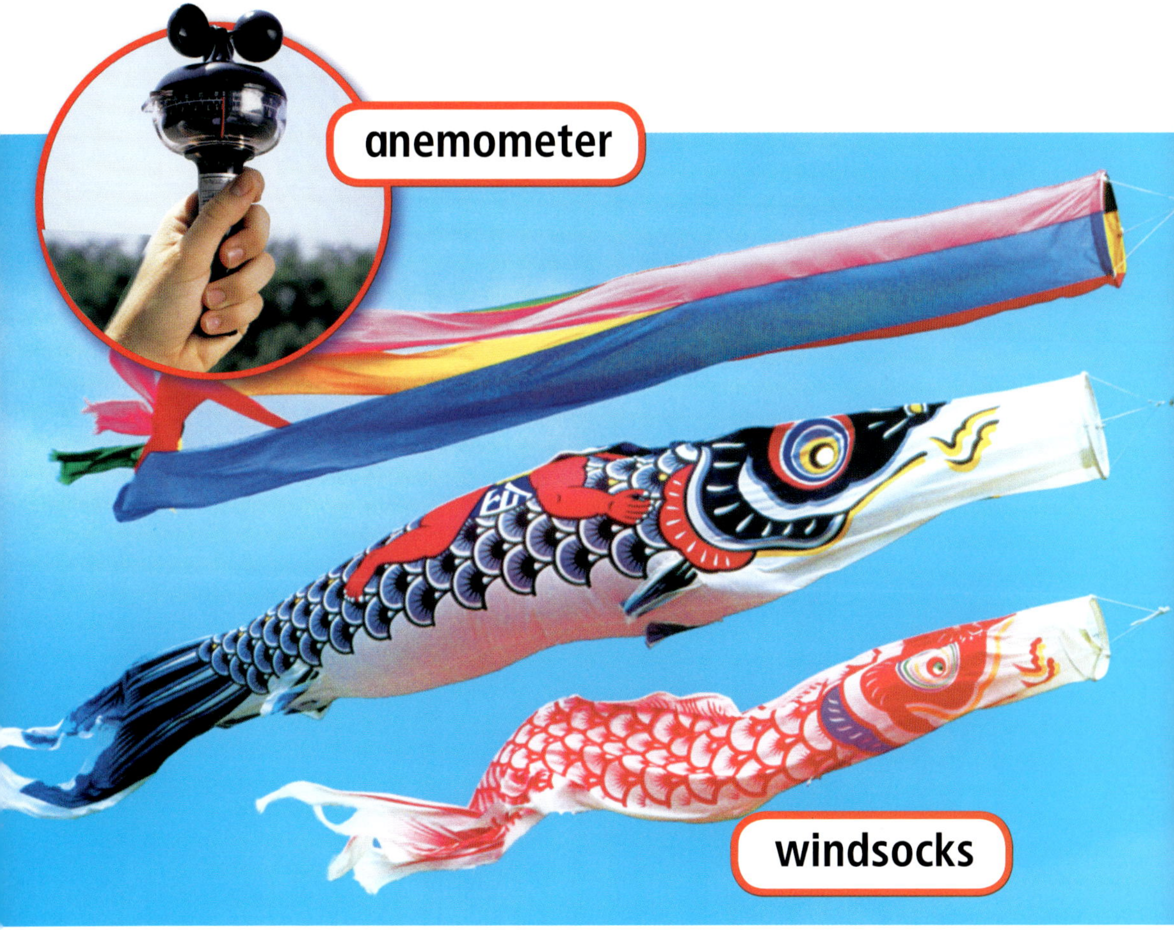

Anemometers measure wind speed. Windsocks show wind direction.

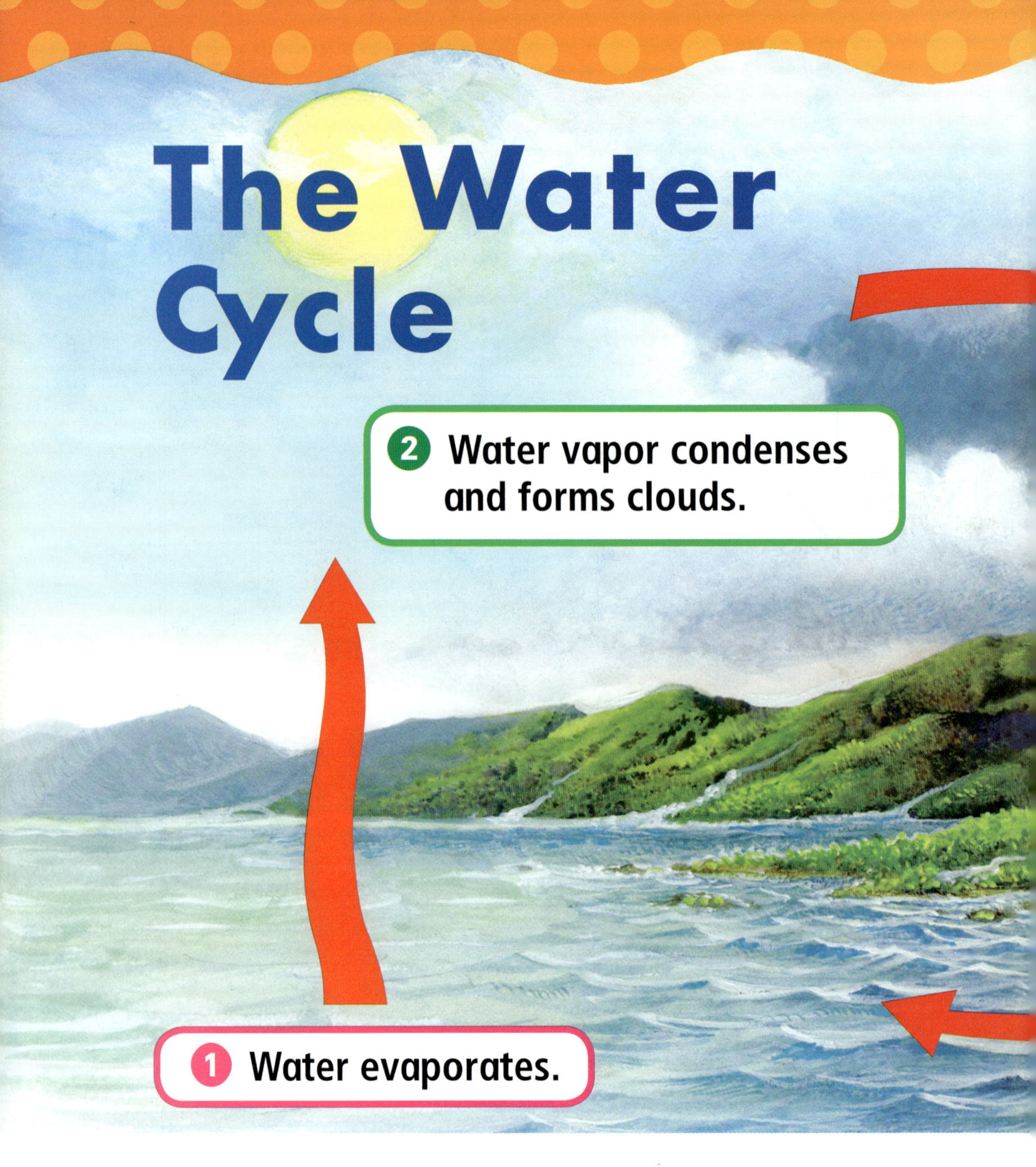

Clouds are part of the water cycle.
Rain is part of the water cycle, too.

Water moves from Earth to the air.
Water in the air falls back to Earth.

Vocabulary

weather, p. 2
temperature, p. 7
thermometers, p. 7
water cycle, p. 10
evaporates, p. 10
water vapor, p. 10
condenses, p. 10